THE GREAT BOOK OF 1967

U.S. Yearbook Full of
Interesting Facts & Events
from 1967

Walter Moore

ISBN-13: 978-1979502245

CONTENTS

INTRODUCTION

The year of the "Summer of Love", 1967 was certainly a memorable one. With an abundance of fascinating circumstances and events, this year is certainly one you'll want to learn about. Let's start here!

In this book, you'll read all about some of the most memorable people and events of 1967. We'll begin by learning about who was in the White House and other important government offices at the time, move on to interesting tidbits about the cost of living, explore an events timeline of occurrences that made 1967 memorable, and talk about celebrities who were born in 1967. And as if that weren't enough, you'll learn about the top music, movies, and books of the year, as well as sports achievements. What a groovy adventure!

PEOPLE IN IMPORTANT POLITICAL OFFICES IN 1967

Lyndon B. Johnson, President of the United States

Everyone's heard of "LBJ", but did you know that he was President of the United States in 1967? Let's learn a bit about Lyndon Baines Johnson, more often known as Lyndon Johnson or "LBJ".

Fun Facts about President Lyndon Baines Johnson

- LBJ occupied the office of President from 1963 to 1969.
- He was a Democrat.
- Johnson's birthday was August 27, 1908.
- He was born in central Texas.
- Johnson was the 36th President of the United States, serving between John F. Kennedy (1961-63) and Richard Nixon (1969-1974).
- Johnson declared his vision to be building "A Great Society" for the people of the United States.
- Lyndon B. Johnson was 64 when he died in 1973.
- In his earlier life, Johnson was elected in 1937 to the House of Representatives

- Before Johnson was President, he was Vice President to John F. Kennedy from 1961 to 1963. He became President when John F. Kennedy was assassinated.
- As President, Johnson successfully got through the enactment of the civil rights bill that John F. Kennedy wanted at the time he was assassinated.

Lady Bird Johnson, First Lady

Chances are that you've never met someone called "Lady Bird" before, but in 1967 the First Lady of the United States had that very name. Lady Bird Johnson was the wife of Lyndon B. Johnson, and therefore the First Lady of the United States. As we all know, this is a tremendously influential position in many ways.

Fun Facts about "Lady Bird" Johnson:

- Lady Bird was named Claudia Alta Taylor at birth.
- She was born on December 22, 1912.
- "Lady Bird" was a nickname but it was the name by which she became best known. The nickname came from a family nurse of her family when she was a child, who said that she was as "pretty as a ladybird".
- Lady Bird Johnson helped finance her husband's first election campaign by drawing from her inheritance.
- When Lyndon B. Johnson eventually became President, Lady Bird became known for her philanthropical

leadership. She worked to alleviate poverty, and supported the important Headstart Program.

Hubert Humphrey, Vice President

Johnson's vice president was Hubert Humphrey, the 38th vice president of the United States.

Hubert Humphrey was born in 1911, in South Dakota. Humphrey was once mayor of Minneapolis, and he eventually ran for the Senate in 1948.

William Ramsay Clark, Attorney General

The U.S. Attorney General in 1967 was William Ramsay Clark. William Ramsay Clark was the 59th Attorney General. He was born in Dallas, Texas in 1927.

John William McCormack, Speaker of the House

John William McCormack was Speaker of the House in the House of Representatives in 1967. He held this office from 1961 to 1971.

A Democrat, he lived from 1891 to 1980. McCormack was born in Boston, Massachusetts.

Earl Warren, Chief Justice of the Supreme Court

The Chief Justice of the Supreme Court in 1967 was Earl Warren. Warren served in this position from 1953 to 1969, when he retired.

Warren lived from 1891 to 1974. He was born in Los Angeles, California. Earl Warren became governor of California in 1943, and he stayed in that position until 1953.

List of Selected U.S. State Governors in 1967

Arizona: Jack Richard Williams (Republican)

Texas: John Connally (Democrat)

California: Ronald Regan (Republican)

New York: Norman Rockerfeller (Republican) (January 1, 1959-December 18, 1973)

New Jersey: Richard J. Hughes (Democrat) (January 16, 1962-January 20, 1970)

Florida: Claude R. Kirk, Jr. (Republican) (January 3, 1967-January 5, 1971)

Michigan: George W. Romney (Republican) (January, 1963-January 22, 1969)

Ohio: Jim Rhodes (Republican) (January 14, 1963-January 11, 1971)

Alaska: Wally Hickel (Republican) (December 5, 1966-January 29, 1969)

North Carolina: Dan K. Moore (Democrat) (January 8, 1965-January 3, 1969)

South Carolina: Robert Evander McNair (Democrat) (April 22,

1965-January 19, 1971)

Minnesota: Harold LeVander (January 2, 1967-January 4, 1971) (Republican)

Alabama: Lurleen Wallace (January 16, 1967-May 7, 1968) (Democrat)

Georgia: Lester Maddox (January 11, 1967-January 12, 1971) (Democrat)

North Dakota: William L. Guy (January 4, 1961-January 2, 1973) (Democrat)

Connecticut: John N. Dempsey (January 21, 1961-January 6, 1971) (Democrat)

New Hampshire: John W. King (January 3, 1963-January 2, 1969) (Democrat)

Massachusetts: John Volpe (January 7, 1965-January 22, 1969 (Republican)

Illinois: Otto Kerner, Jr. (January 9, 1961-May 21, 1968) (Democrat)

Rhode Island: John Hubbard Chaffee (January 1, 1963-January 7, 1969 (Republican)

Maine: Kenneth M. Curtis (January 5, 1967-January 7, 1975) (Democrat)

Idaho: Don Samuelson (January 2, 1967-January 4, 1971) (Republican)

Washington State: Daniel J. Evans (January 11, 1965-January 12, 1977) (Republican)

Mississippi: Paul B. Johnson (January 21, 1964-January 16, 1968) (Democrat)

Wisconsin: Warren P. Knowles (January 4, 1965-January 4, 1971) (Republican)

Oregon: Tom McCall (January 9, 1967-January 13, 1975) (Republican)

Virginia: Mills Godwin (January 15, 1966-January 17, 1970) (Democrat)

West Virginia: Hulett C. Smith (January 18, 1965-January 13, 1969) (Democrat)

Tennessee: Buford Ellington (January 16, 1967-January 16, 1971) (Democrat)

Hawaii: John A. Burns (December 3, 1962-December 2, 1974) (Democrat)

Colorado: John Arthur Lore (1963-1973) (Republican)

Indiana: Roger D. Branigin (January 11, 1965-January 13, 1969) (Democrat)

Louisiana: John McKeithan (May 12, 1964-May 9, 1972) (Democrat)

Montana: Tim M. Babcock (January 25, 1962-January 6, 1969) (Republican)

Oklahoma: Dewey F. Bartlett (January 9, 1967-January 11, 1971) (Republican)

Nevada: Paul Laxalt (January 2, 1967-January 4, 1971) (Republican)

Louisiana: John McKeithan (May 12, 1964-May 9, 1972) (Democrat)

Vermont: Philip H. Hoff (January 10, 1963-January 9, 1969) (Democrat)

Wyoming: Stanley K. Hathaway (January 2, 1967-January 6, 1975) (Republican)

Arkansas: Winthrop Rockefeller (January 10, 1967-January 12, 1971) (Republican)

Delaware: Charles L. Terry, Jr. (January 19, 1965-January 21, 1969) (Democrat)

Kansas: Robert Docking (January 6, 1967-January 13, 1975) (Democrat)

Kentucky: Ned Breathitt (December 10, 1963-December 12, 1967) (Democrat)

Iowa: Harold Hughes (January 17, 1963-January 1, 1969) (Democrat)

Kansas: Robert Docking (January 9, 1967-January 13, 1975) (Democrat)

Maryland: Spiro T. Agnew (January 25, 1967-January 7, 1969) (Republican)

Missouri: Warren E. Heaves (January 11, 1965-January 8, 1973) (Democrat)

Nebraska: Frank B. Morrison (January 5, 1961-January 5, 1967) (Democrat)

EVERYDAY LIFE AND COST OF LIVING IN 1967

The minimum wage in 1967 was $1.40 per hour. The average annual income was $7,300. Luckily, as you can easily imagine, the cost of living was far lower than it is today!

In 1967, a new house cost just $14,250, and average monthly rent was $125. Just $2,750 would purchase you a new car.

Food Prices in 1967

- Freshly baked bread was 22 cents per loaf
- Sugar was 60 cents for 5 pounds
- Milk was $1.15 per gallon
- Coffee was 90 cents per pound
- Fresh ground hamburger was 48 cents per pound
- Eggs were 38 cents per dozen
- Bacon was 74 cents per pound
- Campbell's tomato soup was 11 cents per can
- Oreo cookies were 49 cents per pound
- Kellogg's Corn Flakes were 29 cents per 12 ounces
- A Hershey Bar was 5 cents

Here's a fun list of other 1967 prices:

- The average cost of gas was 33 cents per gallon
- The average cost of a movie ticket was $1.25
- The average cost of a postage stamp was five cents
- A Parker Pen set was $11.95
- A Polaroid camera was $50
- Tuition to Harvard University was $1,855.
- A fireplace screen was $49.95
- A set of five TV trays was $7.99 to $18.99

Most Common Baby Names in 1967

Let's discuss the names that were most commonly bestowed on babies born in 1967.

Girls Names:

1. Lisa
2. Kimberly
3. Michelle
4. Mary
5. Susan
6. Karen
7. Angela
8. Tammy
9. Melissa
10. Jennifer
11. Patricia
12. Amy
13. Elizabeth
14. Christine
15. Laura
16. Julie
17. Pamela
18. Cynthia
19. Donna
20. Sandra
21. Tina
22. Deborah
23. Kelly
24. Lori
25. Stephanie
26. Linda
27. Dawn
28. Teresa
29. Tracy
30. Sharon
31. Brenda
32. Wendy
33. Barbara

34. Denise
35. Cheryl
36. Michele
37. Nancy
38. Debra
39. Rebecca

40. Kathleen
41. Rhonda
42. Maria
43. Theresa
44. Diane
45. Paula

46. Robin
47. Carol
48. Andrea
49. Kim
50. Jill

Boys' Names

1. Michael
2. David
3. James
4. John
5. Robert
6. William
7. Mark
8. Richard
9. Christopher
10. Brian
11. Timothy
12. Thomas
13. Jeffrey
14. Steven
15. Joseph
16. Scott
17. Kevin
18. Paul
19. Daniel
20. Charles
21. Anthony
22. Kenneth
23. Eric
24. Ronald
25. Gregory
26. Stephen
27. Donald
28. Matthew
29. Todd
30. Patrick
31. Edward
32. Gary
33. Douglas
34. Keith
35. Andrew
36. George
37. Rodney
38. Larry
39. Peter
40. Troy
41. Jerry
42. Terry
43. Dennis
44. Sean
45. Frank
46. Craig
47. Jeffrey
48. Raymond
49. Randy
50. Tony

1967 EVENTS TIMELINE — WHAT MADE THE YEAR MEMORABLE

January 2, 1967: Operation Bolo, an air battle

Operation Bolo was an air battle of the war in Vietnam. It was a triumphant act of retaliation for victories gained by the North Vietnamese enemy. F.C. Phantom jets, a brand new model of military plane, were used. The operation began late in the previous year of 1966, but Bolo's D-Day ended up being postponed until January 2, 1967. Operation Bolo is considered to be an important historic event.

January 3, 1967: Ronald Regan became Governor of California

Ronald Regan was born on February 6, 1911 in Tampico, Illinois. He was a famous actor, with a long career in that industry. Regan was in more than 50 movies. Ronald Regan won the election for Governor of California in 1966. He defeated the incumbent Democratic governor, Edmund G. (Pat) Brown, Sr. Regan was the 33rd Governor of California. As most of us know, Regan would eventually become President of the United States in the 1980s.

January 5, 1967: Release of "A Countess from Hong Kong", a film

"A Countess from Hong Kong" is a movie made by Charles Chaplin (better known as Charlie Chaplin), and written by him, too. It is a British comedy, and stars Marlon Brando and Sophia Loren. Charlie Chaplin appears in the movie for a few moments, and it is the last film he ever made.

January 8, 1967 to January 26, 1967: Beginning of Operation Cedar Falls

Operation Cedar Falls was an important operation of the Vietnam Wall. It lasted for a total of 18 days. It involved around 16,000 U.S. soldiers, members of the 11th Armored Calvary Regiment and 173rd Airborne Brigade. They joined 14,000 South Vietnamese troops to carry out the operation.

The operation's purpose was to interfere with insurgent operations that were taking place near Saigon. The Iron Triangle, an area of jungle, and the Thanh Dien Forest Preserve were the targets. The operation resulted in finding and eliminating a tunnel complex situated in the Iron Triangle. It was a headquarters for terrorist attacks and guerilla raids. 488 of the enemy were captured and 711 were killed.

January 14, 1967: The Human Be-In in San Francisco's Golden Gate Park

The Human Be-In attracted more than 20,000 people, and was later considered to be a sort of prelude to 1967's famous Summer of Love. The Human Be-In was primarily a sit-in protest to the Vietnam War. Those who were there were mainly young people and "hippies".

January 15, 1967: The first AFL-NFL Superbowl

The first AFL (which would later merge with the NFL, in 1970) co-existed with the NFL at this time. The first Superbowl, also known as Superbowl 1, was played between the NFL's Green Bay Packers and AFL's Kansas City Chiefs. It took place in Los Angeles.

Most people predicted that the Packers would win, and while The Chiefs did well early on in the game, the Packers ultimately won. Bryan Bartlett "Bart" Starr, a famous quarterback for The Packers, was the star of the day. This is why Starr was given the honor of Most Valuable Player.

January 18, 1967: The "Boston Strangler", Albert DeSalvo, was sentenced to life in prison

Albert DeSalvo, who became known as the "Boston Strangler), murdered 13 women in Boston between 1962 and 1964. He was sentenced to life in prison on January 18, 1967. DeSalvo ended up being killed in prison.

January 20, 1967: "Between the Buttons" by The Rolling Stones released

This album by The Rolling Stones was recorded in Hollywood and at the Olympic Studios in Barnes with Glyn Jones. Some of the songs on the album were started in the United States but completed in the United Kingdom.

The band was able to experiment more than before because of improved recording technology. A critic called Andrew Loog Oldham considered this to be The Rolling Stones' most English album. The album includes songs such as "She Smiled Sweetly" and "Ruby Tuesday". "Between the Buttons" is generally considered to be an extremely important rock album.

January 27, 1967: Three astronauts killed when Apollo 1 caught fire

Three astronauts were killed when the Apollo 1 spacecraft caught on fire. The tragedy happened during rehearsals at NASA's Cape Kennedy.

The fire was likely caused by an electrical spark occurring in the area with support systems such as oxygen supplies. It was because of the oxygen that the fire spread so quickly and killed the crew members in such a short period of time. Apollo 1 has always been remembered as a terrible disaster. The crew included Gus Grissom (the flight commander), Roger Chaffee, and Edward White.

February 1, 1967: Founding of the American Basketball Association

The American Basketball Association was established in 1967. It continued to exist until 1976, when it folded.

The American Basketball Association (otherwise known as the ABA) was meant to be an alternative to the NBA, a league that was supposed to have more of a fun and free-spirited atmosphere. When it first started, the ABA had 11 teams: Oakland Oaks, Anaheim Amigos, Houston Maverick, Denver Rockets, Dallas Chaparrals, New Orleans Buccaneers, New Jersey Americans, Kentucky Colonels, Indiana Pacers, Minnesota Muskies, and Pittsburgh Pipers.

The ABA did not use the traditional orange basketball. Instead, they used one that was red, white, and blue. This and other rather gaudy elements (such as cheerleaders in bikinis) made the league known as a bit outlandish.

February 10, 1967: Ratification of the Twenty-fifth Amendment

The twenty-fifth amendment to the Constitution of the United States was passed in 1967. This amendment sets out rules for succession in relation to vacancies of the office of the president and vice president before a term has expired.

The amendment continued with the already established tradition of the vice president succeeding to the office on the death of the president. It also made a change in that it officially specifies that the vice president would become president if the president resigned. He or she would become the president, not just acting president.

The amendment also specified that if the office of vice president became vacant, the president would nominate a new one (who would need to be confirmed by Congress). The amendment also set out rules for what is to be done if a president lacks the physical and mental ability necessary to fulfill their duties.

March 1967: Jimmy Hoffa sent to prison

Jimmy Hoffa became a labor organizer in the 1930s. He eventually gained the position of president of the Teamsters Union about two decades later. In March of 1967, Hoffa was sent to prison for attempted bribery of a grand juror. The whereabouts of Jimmy Hoffa's body remains a mystery even today.

March 10, 1967: Release of Arethra Franklin's "I Never Loved a Man, the Way I Love You"

Arethra Franklin's "I Never Loved a Man, the Way I Love You" was the singer's 11th album. It was released under the Atlantic record label, and included songs such as "Respect", "Drown in My Own Tears", and "Soul Serenade". "I Never Loved a Man, the Way I Love You" didn't receive a particularly positive review from Rolling Stone when it came out, but it has generally been recognized as an important album in the soul genre.

March 17, 1967: Release of The Grateful Dead's first album, "The Grateful Dead"

The Grateful Dead would become a world-famous band, but at the time they recorded their first album, they knew very little about the recording process. The band was first signed by Warner Bros. Records in 1966. The album contained the songs, "The Golden Road (To Unlimited Devotion)", "Beat It On Down the Line", "Good Morning, Little School Girl", "Cold Rain and Snow", "Sitting on Top of the World", "Cream Puff War", "Morning Dew", "New, New Minglewood Blues", and "Viola Lee Blues".

March 20, 1967: Operation Popeye, a Cloud Seeding Program, is begun by the United States military

Cloud seeding programs sought to change and control the weather, and were meant to be used as tools in warfare (to cause disadvantages to the enemy). These were generally secret programs that were only exposed later on.

March 25, 1967: UCLA triumphs over Dayton in Final Four

This was the 1967 NCAA Men's Division I Basketball Tournament, in which 23 colleges participated. Its purpose was to determine the men's NCAA Division 1's national champion.

The tournament lasted from March 11 to March 25, 1967 (the latter date was the championship game). The tournament involved 27 games total. These included each region's third-place game and a third-place game at the national level. John Wooden was coach to the UCLA team, which won the national title. It has a 79-64 victory over the Dayton team, which was coached by Don Donoher. The Most Outstanding Player of the tournament was given to Lew Alcindor (who later changed his name to Kareen Abdul-Jabbar).

April 1967: Release of The Electric Prunes' first album, "The Electric Prunes"

The Electric Prunes were considered a garage rock band with psychedelic elements. The band formed in Los Angeles in 1964. The Electric Prunes experienced success with the single "I Had too Much to Dream (Last Night) in 1966. In 1967, Reprise Records released the band's debut album, "The Electric Prunes", and another called "Underground".

The Electric Prunes broke up in 1968, while recording another record, "Mass in F Minor".

April 6, 1967 to April 9, 1967: Gay Brewer triumphant at the 31st Master's Tournament

It was quite a surprise when Gay Brewer won the 31st Masters Tournament in Augusta, Georgia. Gay Brewer was from Ohio. He was considered a very minor contender, and his win at the Master's tournament was the only real triumph he had experienced in this career. It is true, though, that the previous year, Brewer had come close to winning the green jacket. He ultimately lost, however, to Jack Nicklaus.

In the 31st Masters Tournament, Brewer managed to beat Bobby Nichols only by a stroke.

April 10, 1967: The 39th Academy Awards

The 39th Academy Awards took place on April 10, 1967. As with all Academy Awards ceremonies, all the nominees and winners were from the previous year. There were many memorable winners, including A Man for All Seasons produced by Fred Zinnemann for Best Picture, Paul Scofield from A Man for All Seasons for Best Actor, Walter Matthau in The Fortune Cookie for Best Supporting Actor, Elizabeth Taylor in Who's Afraid of Virginia Woolf? For Best Actress, Sandy Dennis in Who's Afraid of Virginia Woolf? For Best Supporting Actress, and A Man for All Season's Fred Zinnemann for Best Director.

One particularly memorable feature of the 39th Academy

Awards was the fact that two sisters, Lynn and Vanessa Redgrave, were nominated for Best Actress.

April 21, 1967 to May 16, 1967: Operation Union conducted by United States Marine Corps

Operation Union was an important operation of the Vietnam war. It took place in the Republic of Vietnam's Que Son Valley, and was carried out by the United States Marine Corps.

The Que Son Valley was a very important area strategically, and it was essential that the U.S. forces regain control from facets of the Northern Vietnamese army. Operation Union was a long and difficult operation. At its end, however, the United States' 1st Marine Division won the day and was able to create a permanent base for a large component of its forces in the Que Son Valley.

April 24, 1967: The Hill Fights

The Hill Fights of the Vietnam War began on April 24, 1967. They were not at all well-known at the time. In fact, it took decades for the general public to find out about them. The Hill Fights were fought by United States Marines.

Like many battles and events in the Vietnam War, the Hill Fights were horrific and bloody for the U.S. forces. The Marines found themselves outnumbered by the enemy, as well as outgunned for a large part of the time. The Hill Fights are widely considered emblematic of the general chaos and trauma of the Vietnam War.

April 28, 1967: Muhammad Ali refuses to go to Vietnam

As most of us know, many people (especially the young) rejected the premise and draft of the Vietnam War. The legendary boxer Muhammed Ali was one of them.

At the age of 25, Muhammad Ali was summoned to Houston, Texas, to be inducted into the United States Army after being drafted. He made headlines by refusing to step forward after the calling of his name. He did this as a matter of conscience; he did not believe in the war and was not willing to fight in it. His refusal was a felony offense, with penalties of up to five years imprisonment and a $10,000 fine.

Ali was arrested. While he was convicted, he appealed his case. Ali's license to box in the United States was taken away for three years.

May 2, 1967: Stanley Cup was won by the Toronto Maple Leafs

This was the last time the Stanley Cup has ever been won by the Toronto Maple Leafs. The team has not had such a triumph at any time since. It did win it several times before that, however.

It was a surprise when the Maple Leafs won in 1967, to both their fans and the team itself. The Toronto Maple Leafs had many older players and a few difficult personalities. Also, there was conflict between the team members and the general manager, Punch Imlach.

In the final 1967 Stanley Cup match, the Maple Leafs took on and defeated the Montreal Canadiens.

May 12, 1967: "Are You Experienced?", Jimi Hendrix's first album, released

Jimi Hendrix's debut album, "Are You Experienced?", was extremely successful and became highly influential. Hendrix's genius with the guitar and creativity was immediately recognized.

Jimi Hendrix combined a number of different musical genres including, for example, heavy rock, blues, and psychedelia. The album featured songs such as "Are You Experienced?", "Love or Confusion", and "Foxy Lady".

May 17, 1967: Documentary film on a Bob Dylan tour, "Don't Look Back", was released.

"Don't Look Back" was a black and white documentary film following legendary singer and guitarist Bob Dylan and the people around him on a tour of England in 1965. This popular film was directed by D.A. Pennebake, and featured Bob Dylan and various other fascinating individuals such as poet Alan Ginsberg, Marianne Faithfull, Donovan, and Joan Baez. "Don't Look Back" was 96 minutes in duration, and was shown in cinemas.

May 20, 1967: The Falcon Lake Incident

While this reported encounter with a UFO took place in Canada, it became very well-known in the United States, as well. It happened when a man named Stefan Michalak reportedly encountered a UFO in close proximity to Falcon Lake, Manitoba, Canada.

Michalak said that the UFO's exhaust vent had burned him. He claimed that the UFO made a strange humming noise, had a sulfurous smell, and was well-illuminated. The encounter was investigated by the RCMP. They took soil samples and found radioactivity. The case is still considered unsolved.

May 24, 1967: Release of "Belle de Jour"

"Belle de Jour" was a French film in the drama genre. It starred Catherine Deneuve, a world-famous actress, and also featured Michel Piccoli and Jean Sorel. Deneuve plays a young married woman who works as a prostitute while her husband is out during the day. As can be expected, this film was not without controversy when it was released in the United States.

May 26, 1967: Establishment of the John Fitzgerald Kennedy National Historic Site

The John Fitzgerald Kennedy National Historic site is comprised of JFK's childhood home and birthplace. It is located in Brookline, Massachusetts' Collidge Corner neighborhood.

It was in 1964 that the house was first made a National Historic Landmark, but it wasn't until 1967 that it officially became a National Historic Site.

June 1, 1967: Release of David Bowie's first album, entitled "David Bowie"

David Bowie's first album, "David Bowie", was released by Deram Records. This debut album is known for being markedly different than Bowie's later music, especially with regard to style. In fact, it is known that Bowie was rather embarrassed by this album in some ways, and tried to distance himself from it later on.

June 1967: Robert Henry Lawrence, Jr. became the first African American ever to be an astronaut in the United States

Robert Henry Lawrence, J., was born in 1935, in Chicago, Illinois. He earned a degree in Chemistry at Bradley University, and became a Cadet Commander in the U.S. Air Force. He soon became a full Pilot.

After completing astronaut training and testing, Lawrence became the first African American ever to be in space. This was a historic accomplishment, especially considering the many obstacles that African Americans had to overcome at this time in order to make a career.

Tragically, Robert Henry Lawrence, J., was killed at the age of

32, just months after his historic journey. This happened when he was acting as instructor pilot on a trainee flight of an F-104 Starfighter.

June 1, 1967: The Beatle's eighth album, "Sgt. Pepper's Lonely Hearts Club Band" was released.

"Sgt. Pepper's Lonely Hearts Club Band" was The Beatles' eighth album, and has ended up being one of their most well-known. It is believed that its title was inspired by airplane salt and pepper packets. "Sgt. Pepper's Lonely Hearts Club Band" is admired for its originality and creativity.

June 5 to June 10, 1967: The Six-Day War

The Six-Day War was between Israel and nearby Arab states. Arab states invaded Israel, which was then still only a very young country, hoping to destroy it. This conflict was talked about a great deal in media all over the world.

June 12 to June 13, 1967: Release of film, "You Only Live Twice"

"You Only Live Twice" was a movie in the James Bond series. It was produced by Eon productions. Sean Connery played the fictional character of James Bond, an MI6 agent. James Bond movies were widely popular and generally met with excitement by many. "You Only Live Twice" enjoyed a positive critical reception.

June 13, 1967: The first African-American member of the Supreme Court, Thurgood Marshall, was appointed.

Thurgood Marshall was born on July 2 of 1908, in Baltimore, Maryland. Marshall's father, William, held a job as a steward at a private social club, and his mother taught kindergarten.

Marshall eventually attended Howard University, studying law. After law school, he acted as a member of counsel for the NAACP. He became an advocate for equality for African Americans. Marshall was the lawyer who won the Brown v. Board of Education case that reached the Supreme Court. This led to the elimination of racial segregation in public schools.

Thurgood Marshall was confirmed on August 30th, a couple of months after his nomination was announced. He served on the Supreme court for 24 years.

July 1 to July 14, 1967: Operation Buffalo

Operation Buffalo was an operation of the Vietnam War. it was carried out in the area of Con Thien, in the Demilitarized Zone.

July 23, 1967: The Detroit Riots of 1967

The Detroit Riots of 1967 lasted for five days. 43 people were killed while 342 were seriously injured. 1,400 buildings in the city were seriously damaged or entirely destroyed.

African Americans in Detroit (and around the country) were

suffering from the effects of widespread racism on their lives and opportunities. There was a great deal of anger simmering under the surface. Also, Detroit was beginning to experience serious economic problems.

The Detroit Riots started after police officers raided an illegal bar that was holding a celebration for veterans of the Vietnam war. it was in a poor neighborhood. People in the neighborhood became angry. Within a relatively short period of time, thousands were in the streets. Fires eventually started to break out.

July 29, 1967: Fire on the USS Forrestal

The USS Forrestal was an aircraft carrier. When a fire was caused by explosions, it killed 134 soldiers and injured 161. The aircraft carrier was in the Gulf of Tonkin, on Vietnam War operations. Electrical systems on the ship led to the explosions that caused the fire.

August 2, 1967: Release of "In the Heat of the Night"

"In the Heat of the Night" was a groundbreaking movie dealing with the topic of racism in the Southern states. It was in the mystery drama genre, and was directed by Norman Jewison. "In the Heat of the Night" starred Sidney Poitier, Rod Steiger, and Warren Oates.

August 4, 1967: Release of "Bonnie and Clyde", a movie

"Bonnie and Clyde" was directed by Arthur Penn, and starred Warren Beauty and Faye Dunaway. It was based on the story of Bonnie Parker and Clyde Barrow, the bank-robbing duo from the 1930s. "Bonnie and Clyde" contributed to the popularization of the Bonnie and Clyde story and the legend it engendered.

August 17, 1967: Marriage of Muhammad Ali and Belinda Boyd

In 1967, Muhammed Ali married Belinda Boyd, only 17. She was his second wife. The young woman converted to Islam, and became known as Khalilah Ali. She and Muhammed Ali would eventually divorce in 1967.

August 23, 1967: Birth of Cedalla Marley, daughter of Bob and Rita Marley

Cedalla Marley was one of four children born to Bob, a famous Jamaican musician, and Alpharita Constantia (Rita) Marley. Cedalla would later become a singer and songwriter herself.

August 29, 1967: Cussac close encounter

The Cussac close encounter was a reported alien encounter that took place in Cussac, France and was widely publicized all over the world.

Two children, a 13-year-old named Francois and a 9-year-old named Anne-Marie, claimed they saw four aliens and a glowing sphere or UFO. They said that the UFO smelled like sulfur and made a strange whistling noise.

August 30, 1967: Release of crime film, "Point-Blank"

"Point-Blank" was a movie based on a novel called The Hunter by Richard Stark/Donald Westlake. It is considered by many to be one of the best crime films ever made. Point Blank starred Lee Marvin and also featured Angie Dickinson, Keenan Wynn, and Carroll O'Connor.

September 20, 1967: Release of "The Battle of Algiers", a movie

"The Battle of Algiers" was a dramatic war movie released in 1966 in Europe and 1967 in the United States. Its storyline is set in the 1950s struggle for Algerian independence from France. The movie starred Brahim Hadjadj, Jean Martin, and Yacef Saadi.

October 4 to October 12, 1967: 1967 World Series

The St. Louis Cardinals beat the Boston Red Sox by 7 to 2 in the final game, winning the World Series.

October 21, 1967: The first national demonstration against the Vietnam War.

About 100,000 people gathered at the Lincoln Memorial in a

large protest against the Vietnam War. It was generally a peaceful protest at first. Once the rally before the Lincoln Memorial was done, protestors started marching in the direction of the Pentagon. Some more radical members of the protest got into clashes with U.S. Marshalls that were protecting the Pentagon.

The demonstrators surrounded the Pentagon until early on October 23. Many people were arrested, including well-known individuals such as, for example, the novelist Norman Mailer.

October 23, 1967: Suicide of Helen Palmer

Helen Marion Palmer was born on Sept. 23, 1898. She married Theodor Seuss Geisel (later the famous "Dr. Seuss) in 1927. Palmer was a children's author, like her husband. Palmer's most famous books were *A Fish Out of Water, Why I Built the Boogie House, I Was Kissed by a Seal at the Zoo,* and *Do You Know What I'm Going to Do Next Saturday?*

Helen developed cancer and other illnesses, and was distraught when she discovered her husband had engaged in an affair. She took an overdose of barbiturates and died.

October 25, 1967: Release of "Camelot", a movie

As indicated by the name of "Camelot", this movie was about the British legend of King Arthur, Guinevere, and the knights of the Round Table. Camelot was directed by Joshua Logan, and starred Richard Harris, Vanessa Redgrave, and Franco Nero.

November 1, 1967: Release of "Cool Hand Luke", a movie

"Cool Hand Luke" was a popular movie in the crime and drama genres. It starred Paul Newman, George Kennedy, and Strother Martin, and was directed by Stuart Rosenberg.

November 9, 1967: The Apollo 4 mission

The Apollo 4 mission was a NASA mission also referred to as the Apollo-Saturn 501 (AS-501). It orbited three times, and was an unmanned mission. Apollo 4 launches from the John F. Kennedy Space Center.

November 9, 1967: Founding of Rolling Stone magazine

Rolling Stone magazine was founded on November 9, 1967. As you probably know, Rolling Stone magazine is still published and remains one of the most popular magazines in the world.

November 19 to November 23, 1967: Siege of Dak To

The Siege of Dak To was also referred to as Battle of Dak To. It involved heavy casualties on both the U.S. and North Vietnamese sides. Dak To was located near the Cambodian border, 280 miles north of Saigon.

November 27, 1967: Release of "Magical Mystery tour", an album by The Beatles

This album was the soundtrack of a program called the Magical Mystery Tour, which The Beatles created and directed, and for which it recorded the music.

December 3, 1967: Performance of the first human-to-human heart transplant

The first human-to-human heart transplant took place in Cape Town, South Africa, at Groote Schuur Hospital. The recipient of the heart was Lewis Washkansky, a chronic heart disease patient. The heart used was from a young woman who was killed in a car accident. Surgeon Christian Barnard performed the operation.

December 7, 1967: Heisman Trophy won by Gary Beban

Gary Beban, a UCLA student and football player, was the first player from that college to ever win the Heisman Trophy. The Heisman Trophy is an annual college football award.

December 15, 1967: Collapse of Silver Bridge

The Silver Bridge spanned the Ohio River. It connected Gallipolis, Ohio and Point Pleasant, West Virginia. 46 people died as a result of the collapse.

December 21, 1967: Release of "The Graduate", a movie

"The Graduate" was considered rather shocking when it was released, but that only contributed to its popularity. The movie was directed by Dustin Hoffman, Anne Bancroft, and Katharine Ross. Its director was Mike Nicholas. "The Graduate" remains a popular movie even today, and considered an important contribution to movie history.

CELEBRITIES AND OTHER FAMOUS PEOPLE BORN IN 1967

Julia Roberts: Julia Roberts was born on October 28, 1967 in Smyrna, Georgia. She was the youngest child in her family, and her parents were actors. A top Hollywood actress, she is one of the best-paid people in the movie industry. Julia Roberts got her start in television, on a show called "Crime Story" from 1986-88. In 1988, she starred in a movie called "Mystic Pizza". Her part in "Steel Magnolias" in 1989 led to her being nominated for an Oscar. In 1990, Roberts starred in "Pretty Woman". Julia Roberts went on to star and feature in many other movies, such as Erin Brocovich, for which she won an Oscar.

Nicole Kidman: Nicole Kidman was born on June 20, 1967. In 1990, Kidman featured in the movie "Days of Thunder" and married Tom Cruise, who was also in the film. Nicole Kidman went on to be in a variety of different movies, and to win and be nominated for Academy Awards. In 2002, Kidman won an Oscar for her portrayal of Virginia Woolf in the movie, "The Hours". Kidman and Cruise divorced in 2001. She married

Keith Urban in 2006. Nicole Kidman has a son named Connor and three daughters, Isabella, Faith, and Sunday.

Kurt Cobain: Kurt Cobain was a singer and guitarist, best known for his position in Nirvana, a famous 1990s grunge rock band. Nirvana was extremely popular and successful, but Cobain had to deal with drug addiction as well as depression. He committed suicide when he was only 27 years old. Cobain had a difficult childhood and adolescence, and was bullied at school. Cobain married Courtney Love, another musician, in 1992. They had one child, a daughter named Frances Bean Cobain.

Anderson Cooper: Anderson Cooper was born on June 3, 1967 in New York City. He is the son of Gloria Vanderbilt, a member of the wealthy Vanderbilt family and a successful fashion designer. One of Anderson Cooper's three brothers, Carter, committed suicide in 1988. Anderson Cooper is an investigative reporter and news presenter on CNN. He has his own show, entitled "Anderson Cooper 360". Before Cooper's journalism career, he was an intern for the CIA (Central Intelligence Agency). Anderson Cooper came out as gay in 2012.

Faith Hill: Faith Hill was born on September 21, 1967 in Ridgeland, MS. Hill is a singer in the pop-country genre. She has sold more than 40 million albums. "Take Me as I Am" and "It Matters to Me", her first two albums, achieved multi-

Platinum status in 1993 and 1995, respectively. The singer's first hit song was called "This Kiss". Faith Hill was married to Daniel Hill from 1988 to 1994. In 1996, she married Tim McGraw. Hill and her second husband have three children, Maggie, Gracie, and Audrey.

Mira Sorvino: Mira Sorvino was born on September 28, 1967 in New York City. The actress is the eldest daughter of Paul Sorvino, himself an actor. Mira's first major role was in "Mighty Aphrodite", a Woody Allen movie, in 1995. Sorvino won the Oscar for Best Supporting Actress for her work in this part. Sorvino has featured in many movies and TV shows. She is also known for her support of human rights cause. Sorvino struggled in the first several years of her career. She married Christopher Backus in 2004, and has four children: Mattea, Lucia, Holden, and Johnny.

Dave Matthews: Dave Matthews was born on January 9, 1967 in Johannesburg, South Africa. He is a musician who rose to fame in the 1990s, with The Dave Matthews Band. The band was eventually signed to a major label, and released its debut album "Under the Table and Dreaming", which was very successful. As a child, Matthews' family moved to several different places in the world. His father, who was a physician, died of lung cancer in 1977. Matthews married his wife, Ashley, in 2000. They have three children, Grace Anne, Stella Busina, and August Oliver.

Connie Britton: An actress, Connie Britton was born on March 6, 1967 in Boston, Massachusetts. She was called Constance Elaine Womack at birth. Her father was Allen Womack, a physicist. Her mother, Linda, was a former teacher. Connie's sister, Cynthia, is a fraternal twin. Connie has been in numerous movies and TV shows. She was in several off-Broadway productions early in her career. Connie divorced her husband, John Britton, an investment banker, at the age of 29. They were married four years. Connie became a single mother when she adopted a child from Ethiopia in 2011. His name is Eyob (also called "Yoby").

Jamie Foxx: An actor, comedian, and singer, Jamie Foxx was born on December 13, 1967 in Terrell, Texas. As a child, Foxx was adopted by his maternal grandparents when his parents divorced. Foxx was a member of the cast of the comedy TV show, "In Living Color" in the early 1990s. This established him as an excellent comedian. He grew his career further by proving himself in drama, too. He played Ray Charles in "Ray" in 2004. He won an Academy Award for this role. He also has significant musical talent. Foxx collaborated with Kayne West on the song, "Gold Digger" in 2006. In 2012, Foxx was in "Django Unchained", a Quentin Tarantino movie.

Debi Thomas: Debi Thomas, a famous ice skater, was born on March 25, 1967 in Poughkeepsie, New York. She was the first African American to win a medal in the Winter Olympics (a bronze medal in the Calgary Olympics of 1988), and the women's title at the U.S. Figure Skating Championships. Thomas started skating when she was five years old, and she was winning competitions by the time she was nine. She experienced racial discrimination from judges. Debi eventually went to Stanford University and went on to have a career as an orthopedic surgeon.

Laura Dern: Laura Dern was born on February 10, 1967 in Los Angeles, California. She is an actress, writer, and director. Her parents, Bruce Dern and Dianne Ladd, were actors. Laura Dern is known for her great versatility, and has played many different kinds of parts. Dern's first major movie was "Foxes' in 1980. Many remember Laura Dern in "Jurassic Park", a movie directed by Steven Spielberg.

Will Farrell: Will Farrell was born on July 16, 1967 in Irvine, California. He is a comedian and film and TV actor. Will Farrell's father is Lee Farrell, the keyboardist for The Righteous Brothers, and Kay Farrell, a teacher. Will Farrell was quite and rather studious rather than the class clown in high school. When he graduated from the University of Southern California at Los Angeles in 1989, he became an intern for NBC's sports department. Will Farrell joined Saturday Night Live in 1995, and was wildly successful in the show. Farrell's first movie appearance was in "Austin Powers: International Man of Mystery" in 1997. Will Farrell married Viveca Paulin, an auctioneer from Sweden, in 2000. They have three sons, Magnus, Mattias, and Axel.

Nina Garcia: Nina Garcia was born on May 3, 1967 in Barranquilla, Columbia. Her mother was an actress, while her father was a wealthy importer. Garcia is the fashion director at Marie Claire magazine, as well as a TV personality and writer. Garcia has also been a judge on Project Runway, a TV show, for seven seasons. She studied fashion in both Paris and New York City while a young woman. Garcia became the fashion director at Elle magazine in 2000.

Criss Angel: Criss Angel is a famous magician and TV personality. He was born on December 19, 1967 in East Meadow, New York. He is of Greek-American ancestry. Criss Angel's father owned a donut shop and restaurant. Sadly, he died of cancer in 1998. Criss loved magic from the age of only seven.

Patrick Kennedy: Patrick Kennedy was born on July 14, 1967 in Brighton, Massachusetts. He is the son of Edward and Joan Bennett Kennedy. He is a member of the famous political Kennedy family. Patrick's father was a Senator from Massachusetts. John F. Kennedy was his uncle. He is also the nephew of Senator Robert Kennedy. Patrick was elected to the Rhode Island House of Representatives when he was just 21 in 1988. In 1994, he entered the U.S. House of Representatives for Rhode Island's First District. In May of 2006, Patrick's addiction to prescription medications led to his being admitted to the Mayo Clinic.

Paul Giamatti: Paul Giamatti was born on June 6, 1967 in new haven, Connecticut. He is a well-respected character actor. His first major part was in Howard Stern's "Private Parts", a biopic. Giamatti's father was A. Bartlett Giametti, a former major baseball league commissioner. Some of the movies include "The Negotiator" (1978), "Man on the Moon" (1999), "Planet of the Apes" (2001), and "American Splendor" (2003).

Ana Gasteyer: Ana Gasteyer was born on May 4, 1967 in Washington D.C. She is a comedic actress. Gasteyer's mother was an artist and her father was a lobbyist and later mayor of Corrales, a village in New Mexico. Ana Gasteyer attended Northwestern University's School of communication. In 1996, she joined the cast of Saturday Night Live and became known for her impersonations of Martha Stewart, Hilary Clinton, and Barbra Streisand. Gasteyer left Saturday Night Live in 2002 to focus on a career in the theater.

Jhumpa Lahiri: Author Jhumpa Lahiri was born on July 11, 1967 in London, England. She was born to parents of Bengali heritage. Lahiri's father was a university librarian. Lahiri's first book, a collection of short stories entitled Interpreter of Maladies, was published in 1999. It won the Pulitzer Prize. Her second book was her first novel, The Namesake; it was published in 2003. In the years following, she published more short stories in Unaccustomed Earth. She also published a novel entitled The Lowland in 2013.

Emily Watson: Actress Emily Watson was born on January 14, 1967 in Islington, London, England. Her father, Richard Watson, was an architect while her mother, Katherine (Venables) was an English teacher. She went to university in Bristol to study English literature. Emily Watson has featured in numerous movies and TV productions.

Van Diesel: An actor, producer, and director, Van Diesel was born Mark Sinclair on July 18, 1967 in Alameda County, California. He has a fraternal twin, a brother called Paul Vincent. Van Diesel was a psychologist and astrologer, Donna Sharleen. Van Diesel had an adoptive father, Irving H. Vincent.

TOP MUSIC OF 1967

***The Independent*'s Twenty Greatest Albums of 1967**

1. "Forever Changes" by Love
2. "Sgt. Pepper's Lonely Hearts Club Band" by The Beatles
3. "The Velvet Underground & Nico" by The Velvet Underground & Nico
4. "Are You Experienced?" by The Jimi Hendrix Experience
5. "I Never Loved a Man the Way I Love You" by Arethra Franklin
6. "Songs of Leonard Cohen" by Leonard Cohen
7. "Younger than Yesterday" by The Byrds
8. "John Wesley Harding" by Bob Dylan
9. "Buffalo Springfield Again" by Buffalo Springfield
10. "Disraeli Gears" by Cream
11. "The Doors" by The Doors
12. "Surrealistic Pillow" by Jefferson Airplane
13. "The Piper at the Gates of Dawn" by Pink Floyd
14. "Axis: Bold as Love" by The Jimi Hendrix Experience
15. "Gene Clark with the Gosdin Brothers" by Gene Clark with the Gosdin Brothers
16. "Sell Out" by The Who

17. "Tim Hardin 2" by Tim Hardin

18. "Reach Out" by The Four Tops

19. "Under a Bad Sign" by Albert King

20. "Something Else" by The Kinks

Billboard Year-End Hot 100 Singles of 1967

1. "To Sir with Love" by Lulu

2. "The Letter" by The Box Tops

3. "Ode to Billie Joe" by Bobbie Genre

4. "Windy" by The Association

5. "I'm a Believer" by The Monkees

6. "Light My Fire" by The Doors

7. "Somethin' Stupid" by Frank and Nancy Sinatra

8. "Happy Together" by The Turtles

9. "Groovin" by The Young Rascals

10. "Can't Take My Eyes Off You" by Frankie Valli

11. "Little Bit O' Soul" by The Music Explosion

12. "I Think We're Alone Now" by Tommy James and the Shondells

13. "Respect" by Arethra Franklin

14. "I Was Made to Love her" by Stevie Wonder

15. "Come Back When You Grow Up" by Bobby Vee

16. "Kind of a Drag" by The Buckinghams

17. "Sweet Soul Music" by Arthur Conley

18. "Expressway to Your Heart" by The Soul Survivors

19. "Soul man" by Sam & Dave

20. "Never My Love" by The Association

21. "Apples, Peaches, Pumpkin Pie" by Jay & The Techniques

22. "Come on Down to My Boat" by Every Mother's Son

23. "Incense and peppermints" by Strawberry Alarm Clock

24. "Ruby Tuesday" by The Rolling Stones

25. "It Must be Him" by Vikki Carr

26. "Love is Here and Now You're Gone" by The Supremes

27. "For What It's Worth" by Buffalo Springfield

28. "Gimme Little Sign" by Brenton Wood

29. "The Happening" by The Supremes

30. "All You Need is Love" by The Beatles

31. "Release Me" by Engelbert Humperdinck

32. "Your Precious Love" by Marvin Gaye and Tammi Terrell

33. "Somebody to Love" by Jefferson Airplane

34. "Get on Up" by The Esquires

35. "Brown Eyed Girl" by Van Morrison

36. "Jimmy Mack" by Martha and the Vandellas

37. "I Got Rhythm" by The Happenings

38. "A Whiter Shade of Pale" by Procol Harum

39. "Don't You Care" by The Buckinghams

40. "Then You Can Tell Me Goodbye" by The Casinos

41. "Reflections" by The Supremes

42. "On a Carousel" by The Hollies

43. "Please Love Me Forever" by Bobby Vinton

44. "Alfie" by Dionne Warwick

45. "Silence is Golden" by The Tremeloes

46. "My Cup Runneth Over" by Ed Ames

47. "Up, Up and Away" by The 5th Dimension

48. "San Francisco (Be Sure to Wear Flowers in Your Hair)" by Scott McKenzie

49. "The Rain, the Park & Other Things" by The Cowsills

50. "There's a Kind of Hush" by Herman's Hermits

51. "Mercy, Mercy, Mercy" by The Buckinghams

52. "This is My Song" by Petula Clark

53. "(Your Love Keeps Lifting Me) Higher and Higher" by Jackie Wilson

54. "I've Been Lonely Too Long" by The Young Rascals

55. "Penny Lane" by The Beatles

56. "You're My Everything" by The Temptations

57. "Georgy Girl" by The Seekers

58. "Western Union" by Five Americans

59. "Baby I Love You" by Arethra Franklin

60. "A Little Bit Me, a Little Bit You" by The Monkees

61. "California Nights" by Lesley Gore

62. "Dedicated to the One I Love" by The Mamas & Papas

63. "How Can I Be Sure" by The Young Rascals

64. "Carrie Anne" by The Hollies

65. "(We Ain't Got) Nothin' Yet" by Blues Magoos

66. "Friday on My Mind" by The Easybeats

67. "Soul Finger" by The Bar-Keys

68. "Gimme Some Lovin'" by The Spencer Davis Group

69. "Let it Out (Let it All Hang Out)" by The Hombres

70. "Let's Live for Today" by The Grass Roots

71. "Close Your Eyes" by Peaches & Herb

72. "Groovin'" by Booker T & the M.G's

73. "Funky Broadway" by Wilson Pickett

74. "Pleasant Valley Sunday" by The Monkees

75. "I Never Loved a Man (The Way I Love You)" by Arethra Franklin

76. "Tell it Like it Is" by Aaron Neville

77. "Cold Sweat" by James Brown

78. "She'd Rather Be With Me" by The Turtles

79. "98.6" by Keith

80. "Here We Go Again" by Ray Charles

81. "White Rabbit" by Jefferson Airplane

82. "Bernadette" by Four Tops

83. "The Beat Goes On" by Sonny & Cher

84. "Snoopy Vs. The Red Baron" by The Royal Guardsman

85. "Society's Child" by Janis Ian

86. "Girl, You'll Be a Woman Soon" by Neil Diamond

87. "Ain't No Mountain High Enough" by Marvin Gaye and Tammi Terrell

88. "I Take it Back" by Sandy Posey

89. "Here Comes My Baby" by The Tremeloes

90. "Everything Love" by Robert Knight

91. "I Dig Rock and Roll Music" by Peter, Paul and Mary

92. "I Had Too Much to Dream (Last Night)" by The Electric Prunes

93. "Daydream Believer" by The Monkees

94. "Baby I Need Your Lovin'" by Johny Rivers

95. "Mirage" by Tommy James and the Shondells

96. "Green, Green Grass of Home" by Tom Jones

97. "I Can See for Miles" by The Who

98. "Don't Sleep in the Subway" by Petula Clark

99. "Thank the Lord for the Night Time" by Neil Diamond

Influential Albums Released in 1967

Below are some of the most influential albums released in 1967:

January

January 4: "The Doors" by The Doors

January 20: "Between the Buttons" by The Rolling Stones

January 23: "Miles Smiles" by Miles David

     "Roy Orbison Sings Don Gibson" by Roy Orbison

     "Sugar" by Nancy Sinatra

     "The Youngblood" by The Youngbloods

February

February 1: "Surrealistic Pillow" by Jefferson Airplane

February 6: "Younger than Yesterday" by The Byrds

February 27: "How Great Thou Art" by Elvis Presley

     "There's a Kind of Hush All Over the World" by Herman's Hermits

March

March 6: "Temptations Live!" by The Temptations

March 10: "I Never Loved a Man the Way I Loved You" by Arethra Franklin

March 12: "The Velvet Underground & Nico" by The Velvet Underground, Nico

March 17: "The Grateful Dead" by The Grateful Dead

March 27: "Bob Dylan's Greatest Hits" by Bob Dylan

March 30: "Green, Green Grass of Home" by Tom Jones

April

April 1: "Don't Stop Me Now!" by Cliff Richard

April 29: "The Way I Feel" b y Gordon Lightfoot

    "Happiness is Dean Martin" by Dean Martin

    "The Electric Prunes" by The Electric Prunes

    "Happy Together" by The Turtles

May

May 11: "Are You Experienced?" by The Jimi Hendrix Experience

May 14: "On Stage and in the Movies" by Dionne Warwick

May 26: "Sgt. Pepper's Lonely Hearts Club Band" by The Beatles

    "Live at the Garden" by James Brown

    "Make Way for Willie Nelson" by Willie Nelson

    "You're a Big Boy Now" by The Lovin' Spoonful

June

June 1: "David Bowie" by David Bowie

"Double Trouble" by Elvis Presley

June 2: "From the Beginning" by Small Faces

June 26: "Flowers" by The Rolling Stones

"The Fastest Guitar Alive" by Roy Orbison

"Ray Charles Invites You to Listen" by Ray Charles

"James Brown Plays the Real Thing" by James Brown

"Insight Out" by The Association

July

July 1: "Jigsaw" by The Shadows

July 14: "Bee Gees' 1st" by Bee Gees

July 17: "The Temptations with a Lot o' Soul" by The Temptations

July 24: "Best of The Beach Boys Vol. 2" by The Beach Boys

"Little Games" by The Yardbirds

July 31: "The Everly Brothers Sing" by The Everly Brothers

"Ode to Billie Joe" by Bobbie Gentry

"Reach Out" by Four Tops

"Welcome to My World" by Dean Martin

August

August 4: "Arethra Arrives" by Arethra Franklin

August 5: "The Piper at the Gates of Dawn" by Pink Floyd

August 7: "The Byrds' Greatest Hits" by The Byrds

"Lumpy Gravy" by Frank Zappa

August 27: "I Was Made to Love her" by Stevie Wonder

August 28: "Braded Man" by Merle Haggard

August 29: "Make it Happen" by Smokey Robinson & The Miracles

"United" by Marvin Gaye and Tammi Terrell

August 31: "Cold Sweat" by James Brown

"Goodbye and Hello" by Tim Buckley

"Lush Life" by Nancy Wilson

"The World We Know" by Frank Sinatra

"Carryin' On with Johnny Cash and June Carter" by Johnny Cash and June Carter

September

September 1: "Crusade" by John Mayall & the Bluebreakers

September 15: "Something Else by The Kinks" by The Kinks

September 18: "Smiley Smile" by The Beach Boys

September 25: "Strange Days" by The Doors

"Blowin' Your Mind" by Van Morrsion

"Procol Harum" by Procol Harum

"Everybody Needs Love" by Gladys Knight & the Pips

"Martha and the Vandellas Live!" by Martha and the Vandellas

October

October 10: "Clambake" by Elvis Presley

October 16: "Love, Andy" by Andy Williams

October 26: "Soul Men" by Sam & Dave

October 27: "Where Am I Going?" by Dusty Springfield

October 31: "A Whole New Thing" Sly and the Family Stone

"Silk & Soul" by Nina Simone

"Simply Streisand" by Barbra Streisand

"Pleasures of the Harbor" by Phil Ochs

"Chelsea Girl" by Nico

"Wildflowers" by Judy Collins

November

November 6: "Pisces, Aquarius, Capricorn & Jones Ltd." By The Monkees

November 10: "Days of Future Passed" by The Moody Blues

"Disraeli Gears" by Cream

November 27: "Magical Mystery Tour" by The Beatles

"Someday at Christmas" by Stevie Wonder

"The Temptations in a Mellow Mood" by The Temptations

November 30: "After Bathing at Baxters"" by Jefferson Airplane

"The Butterfly" by The Hollies

"The One and Only" by Waylon Jennings

"Forever Changes" by Love

"The Amboy Dukes" by The Amboy Dukes

December

December 1: "Axis: Bold as Love" by The Jimi Hendrix Experience

December 8: "Their Satanic Majesties Request" by The Rolling Stones

December 15; "The Who Sell Out" by The Who

December 18: "Wild Honey" by The Beach Boys

December 27: "John Wesley Harding" by Bob Dylan

> "Songs of Leonard Cohen" by Leonard Cohen
>
> "13 Smash Hits" by Tom Jones
>
> "A Gift from a Flower to a Garden" by Donovan
>
> "The Look of Love" By Dusty Springfield
>
> "The Magic Garden" by The 5th Dimension
>
> "Sorcerer" by Miles Davis

Selected Band and Artist Profiles

Below is fun and fascinating information on some of 1967's best-known artist and bands!

The Beatles: The members of The Beatles were John Lennon, Paul McCartney, George Harrison, and Ringo Starr. The band first formed in 1960 in Liverpool. The Beatles are regarded as the most important and influential pop and rock group ever to exist. Just a few of their albums include "A Hard Day's Night" (1964), "Yesterday and Today" (1966), "Sgt. Pepper's Lonely Hearts Club Band" (1967), "Magical Mystery Tour" (1967), and "Abbey Road" (1969).

The Beach Boys: The Beach Boys formed in 1961 in California, with the band's original members, Dennis Wilson, Brian Wilson, Carl Wilson, Mike Love, and Al Jardine. One of the stylistic elements the band was known for was its vocal harmonies. The Beach Boys is known as one of the bands most emblematic of the "California Sound" style of pop and rock music. Just a few of the band's albums include "Surfin' Safari" (1962), "Surfin' U.S.A." (1963), "Surfer Girl" (1963), "Surfer Girl" (1963), "All Summer Long" (1964), "Pet Sounds" (1966), "Wild Honey" (1967), "Smiley Smile" (1970), and "Sunflower" (1970). Some of their best-known songs include "Good Vibrations" (1966), "Wouldn't It Be Nice" (1966), "I Get Around" (1964), "Help Me Rhonda" (1965), and "Surfin' U.S.A." (1963).

The Jimi Hendrix Experience: The Jimi Hendrix Experience was formed in Westminster, London in the United Kingdom in 1966. The band's members were Jimi Hendrix, Noel Redding, and Mitch Mitchell. The band continued until Jimi Hendrix died in 1970. The Jimi Hendrix experience released three studio albums, "Are You Experienced?" (1967), "Axis: Bold as Love" (1967), and "Electric Ladyland" (1968). Jimi Hendrix was born in Seattle, Washington, and became known as one of the greatest and most original guitarists to ever live.

The Doors: The Doors formed in Los Angeles in 1965, with members Jim Morrison, Ray Manzarek, Robby Krieger, and

John Densmore. The band's name was inspired by the Aldous Huxley book, *The Doors of Perception*. The Doors released numerous studio albums, including "The Doors" (1967), "Strange Days" (1967), "Waiting for the Sun" (1968), "The Soft Parade" (1969), "Morrison Hotel" (1970), "L.A. Woman" (1971), "Other Voices" (1971), "Full Circle" (1972), and "An American Prayer" (1978).

Stevie Wonder: Stevie Wonder is an American singer and songwriter. Born in 1950, he was a child prodigy and only 17 years old in 1967. Wonder is from Saginaw, Michigan. He suffered from blindness from birth. Just a few of Stevie Wonder's studio albums include "The Jazz: Soul of Little Stevie Wonder" (1962), "Tribute to Uncle Ray" (1962), "With a Song in My Heart" (1963), "Down to Earth" (1966), "I Was Made to Love Her" (1967), "Someday at Christmas" (1967), "For Once in My Life" (1968), "Signed, Sealed, and Delivered" (1970), "Talking Book" (1972), and "Innervisions" (1973).

The Beatles Trivia

When we think of music in the 1960s, The Beatles is a band that inevitably springs to mind. Let's go over some fun trivia about this unforgettable band!

- "Help" was the first The Beatles album to debut at number one.
- The Beatles have spent longer total amount of time on

the Billboard charts than any other band, with 1,278 weeks.

- The Beatles have enjoyed 175 weeks occupying the number one spot on the charts.

- The final live performance of The Beatles took place in Candlestick Park, San Francisco in 1966.

- When John Lennon married Yoko Ono in 1969, he changed his middle name to Ono (from Winston).

- The final album to be released by The Beatles was "Let It Be", while the last album they recorded was "Abbey Road".

- The only two songs to be credited to all four members of The Beatles were "Dig It" and "Flying".

- Not even one member of The Beatles was able to read sheet music.

- While Elvis Presley is history's most famous solo singer, The Beatles are the most popular group.

- The Beatles were the most photographed people of the 1960s.

- Over their career, The Beatles had 17 number one hits in the United Kingdom and 21 in the United States.

- One song written by George Harrison alone was played by The Beatles, during their 1966 tour. It was called "If I Needed You".

- The song "Dear Prudence" was written for Prudence Farrow, actress Mia Farrow's sister.

- "Something", a song by The Beatles, was said to be the greatest love song of all time by Frank Sinatra.
- A 1963 review in the Daily Mirror was the first venue to see use of the term "Beatlemania".
- The Beatles were influenced by many different genres of music, including blues, jazz, folk, and psychedelic rock.
- The Beatles formed in 1960, in Liverpool, England.
- The Beatles most successful songs included "Hey Jude", "Get Back", "She Loves You", "Can't Buy Me Love", "I Want to Hold Your Hand", "Ticket to Ride", "Paperback Writer", "A Hard Day's Night", "Hello, Goodbye", and "Help!".

The Doors Trivia

The Doors was another iconic 1960s band. Let's read some fun The Doors trivia below.

- Jim Morrison, who sang but could not play guitar, was a bit jealous of the band's guitarist, Robby Krieger.
- Jim Morrison was a financial backer of "Themis", his girlfriend Pamela Courson's boutique.
- Jim Morrison had a production company, Hiway Productions.
- "Break on Through" was the first music video ever produced.
- Once at the Aquarius Theater, Jim Morrison swung from ropes like the famous movie character, Tarzan.

- The Doors were the first band to ever use billboard advertising for an album.
- Jim Morrison's father was an admiral in the U.S. Navy.
- Before The Doors were signed by a record company, they were the house band at The Viper Room, an L.A. night club.
- Jim Morrison was 27 years old when he died.
- The Doors' song the "Unknown Soldier" was among the first Vietnam War protest songs.
- The Doors promised not to sing the line "couldn't get much higher" on The Ed Sullivan Show but did so anyway. They were barred from the show as a result.
- The Doors recorded seven albums before Jim Morrison died.

The Monkees Trivia

- Michael Nesmith of The Monkees attended the recording session for "A Day in the Life" from The Beatles' album, "Sgt. Pepper's Lonely Hearts Club Band".
- In 1967, The Monkees sold more albums than The Rolling Stones and The Beatles combined. One big reason for this was the fact that The Monkees had their own TV show.
- Frank Zappa appeared in one episode of The Monkees' TV show.
- The unofficial finale episode of the TV series featured

two The Beatles songs, "Good Morning, Good Morning" and "Hello, Goodbye".

- Two members of the band, Peter Thorkelson and Micky Dolenz, directed episodes of The Monkees' TV show.

- On the night that The Beatles and The Monkees both appeared on the Ed Sullivan show, Davy Jones of The Monkees had never heard of The Beatles

- The Monkees were created with an audition for the "The Monkees" TV series. The band's albums were an offshoot of that. The members of The Monkees only contributed their vocals to the albums.

- "The Monkees" TV series first aired on September 12, 1996 on NBC.

TOP MOVIES OF 1967

The Top 25 Highest-Grossing Movies in the United States in 1967

1. The Graduate

Embassy Pictures/United Artists

Gross earnings: $104,901,839

Budget: $3 million

2. The Jungle Book

Walt Disney Pictures

Gross earnings: $73,741,048

Budget: $4 million

3. Guess Who's Coming to Dinner

Columbia

Gross earnings: $56,666,667

Budget: $4 million

4. Bonnie and Clyde

Warner Bros./ Seven Arts

Gross earnings: $50,700,000

Budget: $2.5 million

5. The Dirty Dozen

Gross earnings: $45,300,000

Budget: $5.4 million

6. Valley of the Dolls

20th Century Fox

Gross earnings: $44,432,255

Budget: $4.69 million

7. You Only Live Twice

United Artists

Gross earnings: $43,084,787

Budget: $9.5 million

8. To Sir, With Love

Gross earnings: $42,432,803

Budget: $640,000

9. Born Losers

American International Pictures

Gross earnings: $36,000,000

10. Thoroughly Modern Millie

Gross earnings: $34,335,025

Budget: $6 million

11. Camelot

Gross earnings: $31,102,578

Budget: $13 million

12. In the Heat of the Night

United Artists

Gross earnings: $24,379,978

Budget: $2 million

13. Casino Royale

Columbia

Gross earnings: $22,744,718

Budget: $12 million

14. I am Curious (Yellow)

Janus Films

Gross earnings: $20,238,100

15. Barefoot in the Park

Paramount

Gross earnings: $19,994,515

Budget: $2 million

16. Wait Until Dark

Paramount

Gross earnings: $17,550,741

Budget: $3 million

17. Cool Hand Luke

Warner Bros/Seven Arts

Gross earnings: $16,217,773

Budget: $3.2 million

18. In Cold Blood

Columbia

Gross earnings: $13,000,000

Budget: $3.5 million

19. Hombre

20th Century Fox

Gross earnings: $12,000,000

Budget: $5.86 million

20. Divorce American Style

Columbia

Gross earnings: $12,000,000

21. Two for the Road

20th Century Fox

Gross earnings: 12,000,000

Budget: $4 million

22. In Like Flint

20th Century Fox

Gross earnings: $11,000,000

Budget: $3,775,000

23. The Trip

American International Pictures

Gross earnings: $10,000,000

Budget: $100,000

24. Doctor Dolittle

20th Century Fox

Gross earnings: $9,000,000

Budget: $17,015,000

25. The Taming of the Shrew

Columbia

Gross earnings: $8,000,000

Budget: $4 million

Popular Actors and Actresses in 1967

Let's look at some of the most popular actors and actresses in 1967.

Warren Beatty

An actor, producer, and writer, Warren Beatty was born on March 30, 1937 in Richmond, Virginia. He and his sister, the actress Shirley McClaine, were the children of a school administrator and a drama teacher. Beatty attended Northwestern University in 1956 and Stella Adler Theater School in 1957. Warren Beatty made his TV debut in 1957 on an NBC show called "The Curly Haired Kid".

Known as handsome and charming, Beatty was known for dating many different actresses, among whom were Faye Dunaway, Julie Christie, Jane Fonda, and Madonna. He did not marry until he was 54, when he became the husband of

Annette Benning in 1992. Beatty has won one Academy Award, and has been nominated 14 times. In 1967, Beatty starred in "Bonnie and Clyde". He also produced the movie.

Rod Steiger

Rod Steiger won the Academy Award for his portrayal of a sheriff in a small Southern town in the 1967 movie, "In the heat of the Night". This is the role by which Steiger is best remembered by many.

Like many other actors and actresses in the 1960s, Steiger practiced Method Acting. Steiger was known for his intensity and versatility. He played a wide variety of parts in both movies and on television including, for example, Al Capone, W.C. Fields, Napoleon, Pontius Pilate, Rudolph Hess, Pope John XXIII, Rasputin, and Mussolini.

Steiger was born on April 14, 1925 in Westhampton on Long Island, New York. His parents were a song-and-dance team. They parted while Steiger was just a baby. Steiger's mother re-married. Unfortunately, the home proved to be unhappy and Steiger left home when he was 15. He enlisted in the Navy when he was 16, lying about his age.

Just a few of the movies in which Steiger starred or appeared include "In the Heat of the Night" (1967), "W.C. Fields and Me" (1976), "Doctor Zhivago" (1965), "On the Waterfront" (1954), and "Al Capone" (1959).

Dustin Hoffman

Dustin Hoffman is a highly respected actor who has become known for playing unconventional characters. He was born on August 8, 1937 in Los Angeles, California. Hoffman's father was a prop supervisor for Columbia pictures and a furniture salesman.

Hoffman dropped out of college when he was 19 years old, and began a career in acting. He became good friends with Gene Hackman, a fellow actor. Dustin Hoffman is quite short in stature for a man and did not have a classically handsome face. His looks made it difficult for him to get roles at first, and he did not get any real breaks for several years.

In the 1960s, Hoffman's biggest movies were "The Graduate", "Midnight Cowboy", and "John and Mary." Eventually Dustin Hoffman won Oscars for his performance in "Kramer vs Kramer" in 1980, and in "Rain Man" in 1989.

Paul Newman

Paul Newman was born on January 26, 1925, in Cleveland, Ohio. In high school, he excelled at football and dreamed of playing it professionally.

Newman appeared in summer stock plays after college, in 1949. It was during this time that he met and married Jacqueline Witts, an actress. Later on, he attended the Yale School of Drama. He was only there a year. He then moved to

New York, and studied at the Actor's Studio with Lee Strasberg.

Paul Newman appeared in many movies in the 1960s, including "Hombre" and "Cool Hand Luke" in 1967.

In the early 1980s, Paul Newman started a food company that gave its profits to charity. It is particularly well-known for its salad dressing.

Rock Hudson

Rock Hudson was born on November 17, 1925 in Winnetka, Illinois. His name at birth was Roy Harold Scherer. When Rock Hudson was a child, his father abandoned the family when he lost his job as an auto mechanic in the Great Depression. Hudson's mother remarried.

Rock Hudson was known for his handsome appearance, and this was a major factor in his entry to the acting profession. He starred in many movies, and co-starred with Doris Day on a number of occasions, such as in "Pillow Talk" (1959), "Lover Come Back" (1961), and "Send Me No Flowers" (1964).

Although it was carefully hidden because of social prejudices at the time, Rock Hudson was gay. He did not come out until 1985, when it was announced that he had AIDS. Sadly, Hudson died that same year.

John Wayne

John Wayne was born Marion Robert Morrison on May 26, 1907 in Winterset, Iowa. Wayne became a famous actor in classic Western movies in the 1940s, 50s, and 60s. He was given the nickname, "The Duke".

John Wayne was married numerous times: to Josephine Wayne from 1933 to 1945, to Esperanza Baur from 1946 to 1954, and to Pilar Pallette from 1954 to his death in 1979. Some of John Wayne's best-known movies include "Red River" (1948), "The Searchers" (1956), "The Man Who Shot Liberty Valance" (1962), "Rio Bravo" (1959), and "The Longest Day" (1962).

Michel Caine

Michael Caine was born on March 14, 1933 in London, England. His father was a porter in a fish market and his mother a charwoman and cook. Caine became known for his Cockney accent.

Examples of movies in which Caine appeared in the 1960s include "Zulu" (1967), "The Ipcress File" (1965), and "Alfie" (1966). He was nominated for an Oscar for his part in "Alfie".

Robert Redford

Known for his handsome looks, Robert Redford was born on August 18, 1936 in Santa Monica, California. His father was originally a milkman but later became an accountant in an oil company. Some of the movies that Robert Redford appeared in during the 1960s included "The Untouchables" (1963), "The Chase" (1966), and "Barefoot in the Park" (1967).

Sidney Poitier

A famous African American actor, Sidney Poitier was born on February 20, 1927 in Miami, Florida. He grew up in poverty in The Bahamas, and later moved to live with his brother in Miami when he was 15. In a time of widespread racism, Poitier became a prominent African American actor in the United States. In 1967, he starred in "To Sir, With Love", "In the Heat of the Night", and "Guess Who's Coming to Dinner".

Anne Bancroft

Anne Bancroft was born on September 17, 1931 in The Bronx, New York City. Her father was a dress pattern maker and her mother, a telephone operator. In 1967, Bancroft played the part of Mrs. Robinson opposite Dustin Hoffman in "The Graduate".

Faye Dunaway

Faye Dunaway was born on January 14, 1941 in Bascom, Florida. She worked as a model before becoming a very successful actress. In 1967, Dunaway starred in "Bonnie and Clyde", "The Happening", and "Hurry Sundown".

Audrey Hepburn

An actress known for her chic sense of style, Audrey Hepburn was born on May 4, 1929 in Brussels, Belgium. Her mother was a Dutch baroness and her father, a businessman. Audrey Hepburn featured in several movies in the 1960s, including the 1967 movies "Two for the Road" and "Wait Until Dark". One of her most well-known films, "Breakfast at Tiffany's", was released in 1961.

Catherine Deneuvre

Known for her French beauty and charm, Catherine Deneuve was born on October 22, 1943 in Paris, France. She featured in many movies in the 1960s. In 1967, she starred in "The Young Girls of Rochefort" and "Belle de Jour".

Brigitte Bardot

A French beauty, Brigitte Bardot was born on September 28, 1934 in Paris, France. Bardot's father worked for his family's business. Brigitte Bardot wanted to be a ballerina when a very young girl. An integral part of the 1960s, Bardot featured in many movies of the decade including, for example, "A Very Private Affair" (1962), "Contempt" (1963), and "Two Weeks in September" (1967).

Natalie Wood

Natalie Wood was born on July 20, 1938 in San Francisco,

California. Her name at birth was Natalia Nikolaevna Zakharenko. Natalie Wood featured in many movies in the 1960s including, for example, "West Side Story" (1961), "The Great Race" (1965), "Penelope" (1966), and "This Property is Condemned" (1966). Natalie Wood started as a child actor, with one of her best known early movies being the Christmas movie, "Miracle on 34th Street" (1947).

Jane Fonda

Jane Fonda was born on December 21, 1937 in New York City. Her parents were Henry Ford, an actor, and Frances Seymour Brokaw, a New York socialite. Jane Fonda appeared in many movies in the 1960s including, for instance, "Sunday in New York" (1963), "Circle of Love" (1964), "The Chase" (1966), "Hurry Sundown" (1967), "Barefoot in the Park" (1967), and "Arabella" (1968).

Julie Christie

Julie Christie was born on April 14, 1941 in Chukua, Assam, India. Her father was a tea planter and her mother, a painter. Christie is of English and Scottish ancestry. Some of the movies in which Julie Christie appeared in the 1960s include "Billy Liar" (1963), "Young Cassidy" (1965), "Doctor Zhivago" (1965), "Fahrenheit 451" (1966), and "Far from the Madding Crowd" (1967).

Mia Farrow

Mia Farrow was born on February 9, 1945 in Los Angeles, California. Her name was Maria de Lourdes Villers Farrow at birth. Mia Farrow's father, John Farrow, was an Australian film director and her mother was Maureen O'Sullivan, an Irish-American actress. Mia Farrow was only about 14 when she started in the industry. In the 1960s, Farrow appeared in "Guns at Batasi" (1964), "A Dandy in Aspic" (1968), "Rosemary's Baby" (1968), "Secret Ceremony" (1968), and "John and Mary" (1969).

BOOKS AND LITERATURE IN 1967

Below are lists of books that were popular with readers in the United States in 1967.

Fiction:

"The Outsiders" by S. E. Hinton

"Endless Night" by Agatha Christie

"The Mimic Men" by V.S. Naipaul

"Rosemary's Baby" by Ira Levin

"Wild Season" by Allan W. Eckert

"The Magic Toyshop" by Angela Carter

"The Chosen" by Chaim Potok

"The Mind Parasites" by Colin Wilson

"Topaz" by Leon Uris

"The Black Pearl" by Scott O'Dell

"I Heard the Owl Call My Name" by Margaret Craven

"The Gab Boys" by Cameron Duodu

"The Owl Service" by Alan Garner

"The Pyramid" by William Golding

"Ice" by Anna Kavan

"Miramar" by Naguib Mahfouz

"Christy" by Catherine Marshall

"Three Tales of Horror" by H.P. Lovecraft

"Picnic at Hanging Rock" by Joan Lindsay

"Deep Waters" by William Hope Hodgson

"Intersection" by Paul Guimard

"Jerusalem the Golden" by Margaret Drabble

"Trout Fishing in America" by Richard Brautigan

"The World that was Ours" by Hilda Bernstein

"Taran Wanderer" by Lloyd Alexander

"The Palace of Love" by Jack Vance

"The Gabriel Hounds" by Mary Stewart

"Strange Gateways" by E. Hoffman Price

"A New Lease of Death" by Ruth Rendell

"Lord of Light" by Roger Zelazny

"The Eighth Day" by Thornton Wilder

"Down These Mean Streets" by Piri Thomas

"Killing Time" by Thomas Berger

"Black Medicine" by Arthur J. Burks

"The Old Man and the Bureaucrats" by Mircea Eliade

"Go to the Widow-Maker" by James Jones

"The Vendor of Sweets" by R.K. Narayan

"The Confessions of Nat Turner" by William Styron

"Flambards" by K.M. Peyton

"The Fox and the Hound" by Daniel Pratt Mannix IV

"Where Eagles Dare" by Alistair MacLean

"The Arrangement" by Elia Kazan

Non-Fiction

"Life Embitters" by Josep Pla

"The Naked Ape" by Desmond Morris

"The Peregrine" by J.A. Baker

"Moral Responsibility" by Joseph Fletcher

"The Death of a President" by William Manchester

"Validity in Interpretation" by E.D. Hirsch

"Augustine of Hippo: A Biography" by Peter Brown

"Beyond Language" by Dmitri Borgmann

"Where Do We Go from Here: Chaos or Community?" by Martin Luther King, Jr.

"The Theory of Island Biogeography" by Robert MacArthur and E.O. Wilson

"The Story of Science in America" by L. Sprague de Camp and Catherine Crook de Camp

Drama

"This Old Man Comes Rolling Home" by Dorothy Hewett

"Edufa" by Efua Sutherland

"Wise Child" by Simon Gray

"Kaspar" by Peter Handke

"Total Eclipse" by Christopher Hampton

"Los Vendidos" by Luis Valdez

"A Day in the Death of Joe Egg" by Peter Nichols

For Children and Young People

"The Giant's Shoe" by Jessica Nelson North

"The Owl Service" by Alan Garner

"Home is the Sailor" by Rumer Godden

"The Great Brain" by John D. Fitzgerald

"A Book of Wizards" by Ruth Manning-Sanders

"When Marnie Was There" by Joan G. Robinson

"Hornblower and the Crisis" by C.S. Forester

"Brown Bear, Brown Bear, What Do You See?" by Bill Martin, Jr.

"Jessamy" by Barbara Sleigh

"Buford the Little Bighorn" by Bill Peet

"Jennifer and Josephine" by Bill Peet

"The Gypsy Game" by Zilpha Keatley Snyder

"The Egypt Game" by Zilpha Keatley Snyder

SPORTS IN 1967

A Timeline of 1967 Sports Memories

January 1: Kansas City Chiefs beat the Buffalo Bills by 31-7 in an AFL (American Football League) championship game. Also, the Green Bay Packers beat the Dallas Cowboys 34-27 in an NFL championship game.

January 9: The name "Saints" is chosen for the NFL New Orleans franchise.

January 15: The first Super Bowl is held, at the Los Angeles Coliseum. The Green Bay Packers triumph over the Kansas City Chiefs 35-10. There is a crowd of 61,946 fans in the stands.

January 18: The 20th NHL All-Star Game is held in Montreal, Quebec, Canada. Montreal beats the All-Stars.

January 21: The AFL (American Football League) Pro Bowl is held. East beats West, 30-23. Also, Peggy Fleming wins the women's title in the Figure Skating championships, while Gary Visconti wins the men's title.

January 22: East beats West 20-10 in the NFL Pro Bowl.

January 23: Stan Musial becomes the Saint Louis Cardinals' general manager.

January 27: The New Orleans Saints sign Paige Cothren-Kicker, their first player.

January 29: Lloyd Waner and Branch Rickey are elected to the Baseball Hall of Fame. Also, Kees Verkerk is named the European skating champion.

February 2: Announcement of the formation of the American Basketball Association.

February 6: Muhammad Ali (Cassius clay) triumphs over Ernie Terrell in Houston, Texas in the fight for heavyweight boxing title.

February 12: Kees Verkerk earns distinction as world champion all-round skater.

February 16: Red Ruffling gains place in baseball Hall of Fame.

February 18: Eddie Feigner, a softball pitcher, successfully strikes out six major league players. Also, Bob Seagren achieves pole vault record, with 17 feet and 3 inches.

February 19: Stien Kaiser gains the title as world champion ladies' skater.

February 22: Border of six feet and sling-shot goal post become standard in the NFL.

February 23: Senator Keith Davey is replaced by Ted Workman as the Canadian Football League commissioner.

March 4: The World Men's Figure Skating Championship is won by Emmerich Danzer of Austria, the World Ladies Figure Skating Championship by Peggy Fleming of the USA, the World Ice Pairs Figure Skating Championship by Ljudmila Belousova and Oleg Protopopov of the USSR, and the World Ice Dance Championship by Diane Towler and Bernard Ford of Great Britain, in Vienna.

March 8: Season tickets begin to be sold by the New Orleans Saints. 20,000 of these tickets are sold on the first day.

March 12: Reinhold Bachler of Austria skip jumps 505 feet.

March 14: In the first NFL-AFL common draft, Bubba Smith is picked by the Baltimore Colts.

March 19: The LPGA Saint Petersburg Orange Golf Classic is won by Marilynn Smith.

March 22: In a Madison Square Garden fight, Muhammad Ali (Cassius Clay) triumphs over Zora Folley, with knock outs in seven innings.

March 25: UCLA wins over Dayton, 79-64 in the 29th NCAA Men's Basketball Championship. Also, UCLA wins the national basketball championship. This is the third time they have done this in four years.

March 26: Kathy Whitworth is the winner of the LPGA Venice

Ladies' Golf Open.

April 2: Susie Maxwell is the winner of the LPGA Louise Suggs Golf Invitational.

April 5: Wilt Chamberlain, a famous Philadelphia '76ers player, sets an NBA record for 41 rebounds.

April 9: Gay Brewer shoots a 280, winning the 31st Golf Master's Championship.

April 14: Billy Rohome, a Boston Red Sox rookie, almost makes a one-hitter at Yankee Stadium, Elston.

April 16: New York Yankees triumph over the Boston Red Sox 7-6 in 18 innings.

April 19: Dave McKenzie of New Zealand wins the 71st Boston Marathon.

April 20: Tom Sayer of the New York Mets is instrumental to his team's victory over the Chicago Cubs, 6-1.

April 21: Los Angeles Dodgers experience their first rain out in Los Angeles for 737 games.

April 23: Kathy Whitworth is winner of the LPGA Raleigh Ladies Golf Invitational.

April 24: Philadelphia 76ers triumph over the San Francisco Warriors in the 21st NBA Championships.

April 28: Muhammed Ali is stripped of his boxing title after refusing to be inducted into the army.

April 30: Tom Seaver, the pitcher of the New York Mets, wins his first game. Also, the LPGA Shreveport Kiwanis Club Golf Invitational is won by Mickey Wright.

May 2: The Toronto Maple Leafs triumph over the Montreal Canadiens, 4 games to 2, in the Stanley Cup.

May 6: Maureen Wilton sets the female world record marathon.

May 7: Carol Munn is the winner of the LPGA Tall City Golf Open.

May 13: Mickey Mantle of the New York Yankees hits the 500th home run of his career.

May 15: Jo Ann Prentice is the winner of the LPGA Dallas Citivan Golf Open.

May 21: LPGA Babe Didrikson-Zaharies Golf Open is won by Marilynn Smith.

May 24: The Cincinnati Bengals are granted a franchise by the AFL.

May 25: The 12th Europe Cup is won by Celtic, in Lisbon.

May 30: Almost 41 years old, Whitney Ford of the New York Yankees announces that he is retiring from baseball.

June 12: In 22 innings, the Washington Senators beat the Chicago White Sox, 6-5.

June 20: The New York Mets is defeated by the Philadelphia

Phillies' Larry Jackson.

July 8: A bowling record of 4,585 in 24 games is set by Helen Weston of Detroit, Michigan. Also, Billie Jean King wraps up her Wimbledon sweep.

July 11: The National League triumphs over the American League in the Longest All-Star game.

July 12: The New York Mets beat the New York Yankees in the 5th Mayor's Trophy Game.

July 14: Eddie Matthews of the Houston Astros hits his 500th home run.

July 26: In 18 innings, the Minnesota Twins beat the New York Yankees.

August 5: The Denver Broncos beat the Detroit Lions by 13-7, the first time an AFL team ever beats an NFL one.

August 18: Tony Conigliaro of the Boston Red Sox is seriously injured, his left cheekbone shattered by a fastball. He misses the remainder of the 1967 season, as well as the entire 1968 one.

August 25: Dean Chance of the Minnesota Twins is instrumental to the team's triumph over the Cleveland Indians.

September 1: in 21 innings, the San Francisco Giants beat the Cincinnati Reds 1-0.

September 17: In the team's first NFL game, the New Orleans

Saints lose to the Los Angeles Rams, 27-13.

September 22: Pitcher Dallas Green, the team's future manager, is released by the Philadelphia Phillies.

September 24: Jim Bakken of the Saint Louis Cardinals achieves seven field goals in a game with the Pittsburgh Steelers.

October 4: The first World Series not to involve the New York Yankees, Los Angeles Dodgers, or San Francisco Giants since 1948, is held.

October 12: In the 64th World Series, the Saint Louis Cardinals beat the Boston Red Sox.

October 23: The New Jersey Americans (who would later become the New Jersey/New York Nets) take part in their first ABA game.

November 5: The New Orleans Saints beat the Philadelphia Eagles, achieving their fist NFL victory.

December 1: Wilt Chamberlain achieves 22 free throw misses, setting an NBA record. Also, one of two American League expansion franchise teams (Seattle) is awarded to Pacific Northwest Sports.

December 3: Derek Clayton achieves a world record marathon.

December 8: The Oakland Seals becomes the new name of the NHL's California Seals.

December 13: The National Pro Soccer League and United Soccer Association merge into NASL.

December 31: In a NFL championship game, the Green Bay packers beat the Dallas Cowboys, 21-17. In an AFL championship game, the Houston Oilers are defeated by the Oakland Raiders, 40-7. Also, the Houston Rockets are defeated by the Los Angeles Lakers at the first NBA game at the Great Western Forum.

Football in 1967

- The first Superbowl was held on January 15th. The Green Bay Packers, the NFL champion, beat the Kansas City Chiefs, the AFL champion, 35-10.
- The Houston Oilers are defeated by the Oakland Raiders in the 1967 American Football League Championship, 40-7.
- The New Orleans Saints are established as a team.
- On the last day of the year, the Green Bay Packers beat the Dallas Cowboys, 21-17.

Basketball

- The American Basketball Association becomes the NBA's rival league.
- The San Francisco Warriors are defeated by the Philadelphia 76ers, 4 games to 2.
- UCLA beats Dayton, 79-64.

- The Philadelphia 76ers beat the San Francisco Warriors to win the series.

Golf

- The Ryder Cup is won by the United States, beating Britain.
- The PGA Tour's money leader is Jack Nicklaus, at $188,998.
- The PGA Championships are won by Don January.
- The British Open is won by Roberto DeVicenzo.
- The U.S. Open is won by Jack Nicklaus.
- The Masters Tournament is won by Gay Brewer.
- The LPGA's Tour money leader was Kathy Whitworth, at $32,937.
- The U.S. Women's Open winner is Catherine Lacoste.
- The LPGA Championship is won by Kathy Whitworth.
- The Women's Western Open is won by Kathy Whitworth.

Baseball

- The Kansas City Athletics are determined to be the Oakland Athletics for 1968.
- In the World Series, the St. Louis Cardinals beat the Boston Red Sox by four games to three. Bob Gibson, a pitcher, is the series MVP.

Ice Hockey

- Six new ice hockey teams were added by the NHL for

the 1967-68 season.

- During the NCAA Men's Ice Hockey championship, Cornell University's Big Reds beat Boston University Terriers, 4-1, in Syracuse, New York.

- In the World Hockey Championship, the Soviet Union beat Sweden in the men's division.

- In the Hart Memorial Trophy, Stan Mikita of the Chicago Black Hawks won for the NHL's Most Valuable Player.

- Stan Mikita of the Chicago Black Hawks wins the Art Ross Trophy as the leading scorer in the regular season in the NHL.

- For the Stanley Cup, the Toronto Maple Leafs beat the Montreal Canadiens, four games to two.

Swimming

- On October 8, 1967, Mark Spitz again achieved the world record in the 200m butterfly course in West Berlin, West Germany. Earlier that year, John Ferris, another American swimmer, had taken the record. It was on July 26 of 1967 that Mark Spitz originally set the record in this area.

Soccer

- The Los Angeles Wolves won the championships of the United Soccer Association.

The Green Bay Packers Roster for 1967

Below is a list of the players of the Green Bay Packers in 1967, when the team won the Superbowl.

Herb Adderley	Don Hom
Lionel Aldridge	Bob Hyland
Donny Anderson	Claudis James
Ken Bowman	Bob Jeter
Zeike Bratkowski	Henry Jordan
Allen Brown	Ron Kostelnik
Robert Brown	Jerry Kramer
Tom Brown	Bob Long
Lee Roy Caffrey	Max McGee
Dick Capo	Ray Nitschke
Don Chandler	Eliah Pitts
Tommy Crutcher	Dave Robinson
Carroll Dale	John Rowser
Willie Davis	Bob Skoronski
Boyd Dowler	Bart Starr
Jim Flanigan	Fuzzy Thurston
Mary Fleming	Jim Weatherwax
Gale Gillingham	Travis Williams
Jim Grabowski	Ben Wilson
Forrest Gregg	Willie Wood
Doug Hart	Steve Wright

1967: WHAT A YEAR!

There's one thing almost all of us will agree with – 1967 was an extraordinary and historic year. It led to a great deal of social change and fascinating developments in the United States and around the world. Some of its greatest accomplishments were in the areas of popular culture, with tremendously influential music, movies, and books. We hope that you've enjoyed this Great Book of 1967, and been able to imagine what life was like many decades ago.